Date: 9/17/20

BR 636.76 SCR
Scragg, Hailey,
Yorkshire terrier puppies /

Table of Contents

Rourke
Educational Media

A Division of
Carson
Dellosa
Education

rourkeeducationalmedia.com

Can you find these words?

ears

nap

puppies

run

Yorkshire Terrier Puppies

puppies

These are Yorkshire Terrier **puppies**! They are called Yorkies.

ears

What do Yorkie puppies look like?

4

They have pointy **ears**.

5

Their hair is long and soft.

6

What do Yorkie puppies act like?

They like to **run** and play.

run

They want their own way.

This puppy wants the brush!

They need lots of sleep.

They like to **nap.**

nap

Did you find these words?

They have pointy **ears**.

They like to **nap**.

These are Yorkshire Terrier **puppies**!

They like to **run** and play.

Photo Glossary

 **ears** (eerz): The organs you hear with on either side of the head.

 **nap** (nap): To sleep for a short time, often during the day.

 **puppies** (PUHP-eez): Dogs that are young and not fully grown.

 **run** (ruhn): To move faster than a walk.

Index

About the Author

Hailey Scragg is a writer from Ohio. She loves all puppies, especially her puppy, Abe! She likes taking him on long walks in the park.

www.rourkeeducationalmedia.com

PHOTO CREDITS: cover: ©JLSnader, manley099 (bone); back cover: ©speeple22 (inset), ©Naddiya (pattern); pages 2, 3, 14, 15: ©anetapics; pages 2, 4-5, 14, 15: ©Scorpp; pages 6-7: ©KPG Payless2; pages 2, 8-9, 14, 15: ©STOWEN SETO; pages 10-11: ©Anna Efimova; pages 2, 12-13, 14, 15: ©lillisphotography

Edited by: Kim Thompson
Cover and interior design by: Janine Fisher

Library of Congress PCN Data
Yorkshire Terrier Puppies / Hailey Scragg
(Top Puppies)
ISBN 978-1-73162-868-8 (hard cover)(alk. paper)
ISBN 978-1-73162-867-1 (soft cover)
ISBN 978-1-73162-880-0 (e-Book)
ISBN 978-1-73163-343-9 (ePub)
Library of Congress Control Number: 2019945493

Printed in the United States of America,
North Mankato, Minnesota